W9-AKU-814

Birds' Nests

Written by Eileen Curran

Illustrated by Pamela Johnson

Troll Associates

Library of Congress Cataloging in Publication Data

Curran, Eileen.
  Birds' nests.

  Summary: An introduction to birds' nests in simple
language, explaining where and why they are built.
    1. Birds—Nests—Juvenile literature. [1. Birds—
Nests] I. Johnson, Pamela, ill. II. Title.
QL675.C87   1985   598.2'564   84-8658
ISBN 0-8167-0341-8 (lib. bdg.)
ISBN 0-8167-0342-6 (pbk.)

Copyright © 1985 by Troll Associates, Mahwah, New Jersey
All rights reserved. No part of this book may be used
or reproduced in any manner whatsoever without written
permission from the publisher.
Printed in the United States of America

10 9 8 7 6 5 4 3 2 1

Canada Geese

Common Flickers

Woodpeckers

High in the sky...
up in the trees.

Wied's Crested Flycatcher

Ring-Billed Gull

Mallard Duck

Bluebird

Rivoli's Hummingbird

Acorn Woodpecker

Snowy Owl

There are all kinds of birds.
Here they come now.

High in the branches.

White-Throated Sparrow

Indigo Bunting

Up in the trees.

Black-Capped Chickadee

Chipping Sparrow

They build their nests.

Prothonotary Warbler

Cardinals

They build their homes.

Robin

Ruffed Grouse

Swallows

High near a rooftop.
Look up and see.

This bird makes a nest...

Swallow

1

2

3

4

...from mud and straw.

Down in the reeds.

Common Terns

Look and see.

Baltimore Oriole

Female Baltimore Oriole

This bird makes a nest...

Male Baltimore Oriole

...that hangs from a tree.

Baya Weavers

Some birds *weave* their nests.

Giant Grebe

Other nests can *float*.

Bald Eagles

Peregrine Falcons

Why do birds build nests?
What are they for?

Sparrow Hawk

*Great Horned
Owls*

Robin

Warbler

Nests keep eggs safe.

Blue Jay

Woodpecker

They help keep eggs warm.

Flickers

Robin

Now the eggs hatch.

Bittern

The babies are born!

Ducks

Robins

High in the sky.

Up in the trees.

Cedar Waxwings

Cock-of-the-Rock

Ariel Toucans

Soon the babies try to fly.

Macaws

Thick-Billed Parrots

Can they do it?

Roseate Spoonbills

Yes, they will!
Look up and see.